Vinh Liem

Without Beginning Without End
Poetry

Lulu
2008

Without Beginning Without End – Poetry
By **Vinh Liem**

Library of Congress Catalog Card Number:
International Standard Book Number: 978-0-6152-0497-0

Table of Contents

Preface

Since I came to the United States in 1975 as a refugee, I never thought that I would have an opportunity to publish my poems in English. Although I wrote some poems directly in English, I was not sure that those poems would carry the poetical sound as it did in my native language – Vietnamese.

Some of my poems in this book were selected from the originals, which were written in Vietnamese. They were translated into English by Mr. Huynh Sanh Thong (a Vietnamese scholar at Yale University), Dr. Ralph S. Carlson (an English Professor at Azusa Pacific University, Azusa, California), and Mr. Nguyen Ngoc Bich (Scholar, Virginia). Most of them were written directly in English in the mid 70's, 80's, 90's and 00's. One poem, which I wrote in English, was translated into German by Dr. T.L. Eichman (an English Professor at Montgomery College, Takoma Park, Maryland).

In 1980, I attended Montgomery College at Takoma Park as a part-time student. One day I gave my poem – *One Day Will Come*[1] – to my English instructor, Dr. T. L. Eichman, and asked for his suggestions. In the next class meeting, Dr. Eichman handed me a piece of paper and told me that he translated my poem into German.[2] I then sent the translation to my friends in West Germany, who published a Vietnamese magazine called Doc Lap. That translation – Eines Tages Kommt Es – was published in the issue of the Vietnamese New Year, in 1982.

---

[1] See page 1.
[2] See *'Eines Tages Kommt Es'* on page 3.

From 1980 to 1982, Mr. Huynh Sanh Thong translated some of my poems into English. One of these poems was printed in *The Vietnam Forum,*[3] a review of Vietnamese culture published in 1983 by Southeast Asia Studies, part of Yale University. Another poem was printed in *'A Break in the Clouds.'*[4] published by The National Library of Poetry.

In 1984, I met Dr. Ralph S. Carlson (aka Le Kinh Kha) at a meeting in Washington, D.C. and I gave him a book of my poems.[5] After returning to California, a couple of weeks later, Carlson sent me his draft and asked me for advice. He liked my poems a lot. Carlson translated most of my poems and a narrative poem in that book.[6] One of these poems was printed in *'War and Exile.'*[7] Another poem was printed in *'At Day's End.'*[8] published by The National Library of Poetry.

My poems (written in English) were published in *'Divining Beauty'* (2001) by The National Library of Poetry in Owing Mills, Maryland and in *'Theatre of The Mind'* (2003) by Noble House in the UK. One poem (*'Enemy'*) was recorded in *'The Sound of Poetry'*, released both on compact disk and cassette tape in Fall 2001, by The International Library of Poetry.

If you have any suggestions or comments, please let me know. I appreciate your time. You can contact me on vinhliem9@hotmail.com

---

[3] Vinh Liem, *'Chatting with my old schoolteacher,'* The Vietnam Forum, Southeast Asia Studies, Yale University (Winter-Spring 1983): 108-110.

[4] *'A Break in the Clouds,'* The National Library of Poetry. Owings Mills, Maryland (1983).

[5] Vinh Liem, *'Bi Ca Nguoi Vuot Bien'* (a book of poems written in Vietnamese). Con Rong Books. Silver Spring, Maryland (1980).

[6] See *'Lament of the Boat People'* to be published in 2008 by Lulu.

[7] Vinh Liem, *'Ko Kra,'* War and Exile – A Vietnamese Anthology. Vietnamese PEN Abroad (1989): 218-219.

[8] *'At Day's End,'* The National Library of Poetry. Owings Mills, Maryland (1994).

Acknowledgments

I would like to give special thanks to the following translators who contributed to this edition: Mr. Huynh Sanh Thong, Yale University; Dr. Ralph S. Carlson, Azusa Pacific University (California); Dr. Thomas L. Eichman, Montgomery College at Takoma Park (Maryland); and Mr. Nguyen Ngoc Bich (Virginia).

I am also indebted to those who cheerfully read and gave me their thoughtful suggestions: Joan Marie Sutton (St. Louis, Missouri); Sara Reavin, novelist (Rockville, Maryland); Colonel Samuel Shumaker, Ret., Columbia Union College (Takoma Park, Maryland); Dr. Alayne Thorpe, Columbia Union College (Takoma Park, Maryland); and Douglas Burke, a freelance writer (Takoma Park, Maryland).

Carlie Lee from Pen Friends UK (www.pefruk.co.uk), special thanks for her proofreading efforts.

Germantown, October 31, 2000 (My 25th Halloween)
Revised on April 8, 2007 & January 15, 2008

Vinh Liem

Books published in the United States

1. **Ti Nan Truong Ca I** (Refugee's Confidences) – Book of poems, Vol. I, written in Vietnamese, published in 1980
2. **Bi Ca Nguoi Vuot Bien** (Lament of the Boat People) – Book of poems written in Vietnamese, published in 1980
3. **Ti Nan Truong Ca II** (Refugee's Confidences) – Book of poems, Vol. II, written in Vietnamese, published in 1980
4. **Ga Ti Nan** (The Refugee Guy) – A collection of short stories written in Vietnamese, published in 1986

Community and Organization Activities:

1999 – 2002	Acting Chairman of Association of Free Vietnamese Writers and Artists
1995 – 2001	Coordinator of Democracy for a Free Vietnam
1995	Coordinator, April 30th Commemoration Committee
1994 – 1995	Coordinator of Committee for Defending the National Cause
1993 – 1999	Chairman of Association of Free Vietnamese Writers and Artists
1993 – 1995	Member of The Standing Committee, Vietnamese Community at MD-DC-VA
1992 – 1995	President of Vietnamese ISAW Committee
1989 – 1995	Founder and President of Vietnamese Overseas Experts and Youth Association
1981 – 2001	Founder and President of Viet Club, Inc.
1980 – 1993	Member of Vietnamese Pen Club Overseas
1980 – 1990	Member of Young Republican, Maryland
1980 – 1986	Vice President of Vietnamese Communities Overseas
1976 – 1979	Co-Founder and General Secretary of Vietnamese Community at St. Louis, Missouri

One Day Will Come

I have been here in a strange country;
My heart is sad — without family, with no happiness!
I don't know why I'm here!
My life has been full of tears.

Three years have passed since 1975.
I have opened my eyes,
To see what will happen in my future.
I feel unlucky, just like a failure!

Who gave my country away to the communists?
So many men arrived here without their kids!
They dream every day and every night,
About the family reunion with their wives.

I love my country just the same as I do my parents,
There, I can have everything I want.
My mother cooking me good food and making my
*   clothes;*
And bringing to me the family life I really enjoy.

Now everything is so far away.
The new life has changed the Vietnamese every day.
They have to live without hope, medicine, clothes and
      food.
Do you think that communism is still good?

I wish I could return home some day,
We will enjoy freedom that we pray.
My parents will say: 'Hello my good boy!'
I will then kiss my children and my wife.

(St. Louis, Sept. 10, 1978)

Eines Tages Kommt Es

Ich bin in einem fremden Land;
Es trauert mir das Herz — ohne Verwandten, ohne
    Glück !
Ich weiss nicht, warum ich da bin !
Mir ist das Leben tränenvoll.

Drei Jahre sind seit 1975 vergangen.
Ich habe die Augen geöffnet,
Um zu sehen, was mir die Zukünft bringt.
Ich fühle mich glücklos, genau wie ein Taugenichts.

Wer gab mein Land den Kommunisten?
So viele kamen ohne Kinder hierher!
Sie träumen Tag und Nacht
Von dem Wiedersehen mit den Frauen.

Ich liebe mein Land so sehr wie ich die Eltern liebe,
Dort kann ich alles Erwünschte haben,
Die Mutter mir Gutes kochen, Kleider machen,
Und mir die Familie bringen, die mir so gefällt.

Nun ist alles fern von hier.
Das neue Leben verwandelt die Vietnamesen jeden Tag.
Sie müssen ohne Hoffnung, Medizin, Kleider und Essen
     leben.
Glaubst du, daß die Kommunisten so gut seien?

Ich wünsche, ich könnte eines Tages zur Heimat
     wiederkehren.
Gott wird uns die Freiheit in die Hand geben.
Meine Eltern werden sagen, "Hallo, guter Bub!"
Ich werde dann meine Kinder und Frau küssen.

(St. Louis, Sept. 10, 1978)

(Übersetzt von Dr. T. L. Eichman)

Why Have We Stayed Here?

Why have we stayed here?
Our eyes have no more tears.
We cried a lot in the past!
Nobody can answer best.

Why we have stayed here?
Don't you read the newspapers?
They showed you our lesson;
We're not the poor citizens.

Why have we stayed here?
Don't you believe what we fear?
In hands of the communists
Poor are our people indeed.

Why have we stayed here?
Our people die every day.
The big prison we have to face!
'Political reason' that we hate.

Why have we stayed here?
How can we live without care?
Without meeting and no free press.
No Human Rights at all, you can guess!

Why have we stayed here?
Although we have good ideas
Yet we have no more thoughts!
All we do is to keep our mouths shut!

Why have we stayed here?
We heard the Liberty in many years
Just as you feel and hope.
We are here — not for food or work!

Why have we stayed here?
Live free here or die easy there.
Prices of Freedom and Democracy;
They're too expensive, not free!

(St. Louis, Sept. 10, 1978)

Inspiration

(For Joan Marie Sutton)

I never thought I'd meet you,
At a wedding party on the hill.
Would I be happy and very kind?
Because you did give me a smile.

Hand in hand you said you liked me;
Eye to eye showed what it would be.
My loneliness had gone away.
Oh my dear! What did you say?

The short time I spent with you,
And for the first time I knew
I learned a lot about your world.
It made me feel I wasn't alone.

Since I've been in this country,
Without relatives and my family.
I'm as free as a dove;
Would you mind giving me your love?

My life was as sad as an empty house;
I felt like a horse living in a town;
I didn't know what to do —
No sign to go; no place to move.

I lie on my bed; eyes open wide.
An inspiration comes to my mind.
For the first time I'm thinking of you;
And for the first time, I'll tell you the truth.

(St. Louis, Sept. 10, 1978)

Chatting With My Old Schoolteacher

The restive horse, alive and kicking yet,
set off to travel, following the times.
He meant to see new lands and thus forget –
but towards his country he still turns his gaze.

He thirsts for contact with some kindred soul.
He craves the scent he smelled in soft, smooth hair.
Oh, how he dreams of gleaming eyes far off,
of that hot breath which burned his heart, his guts.

He toils and moils, surrounded by a world
of strangers who avert their eyes, their ears.
A man must hustle, scrounging food and clothes,
forever doomed to play the hanger-on.

His old schoolteacher's now bow-backed, gray-haired—
along the eyelids linger cares and grievances.
He had his heyday swaggering—oh, it's gone!
But what on earth have those two hands achieved?

The teacher shyly clasps the student's hand.
What wind has blown us two together here?
We wanderers meet abroad—it's joy enough.
You must feel sad about an exile's life.

Past days and months are stirring in your mind.
You miss your youth, long for those verdant years.
Your feet trod jungles, trampled red-hued earth—
"The people's revolution!" cried your mouth.

When "revolution' came, why did you flee?
You knew all Marxist-Leninist thought by heart.
So many adolescents you destroyed—
do you feel happy now on alien soil?

A college campus bored the restive colts—
he spurned young grass that felt so cool, smelled fresh.
He donned a red beret and roamed the wilds,
With the love of his fair homeland in his heart.

For "revolution," joining its marquis,
some hoped to mend the heavens like Nü Wa.[1]
Uncowed by bullets, they all sallied forth—
but manly grit could just hold out a while.

Some looked down on an officer's stripes, stayed home
and learned the way of life from Bachelor Xuong.[2]
Religion others chose, becoming monks,
eschewing love and all its earthly scents.

How can I tell them all, things past and gone?
Such grievances and woes! Enough to fill a sea.
If outwardly I live, within I'm dead—
the world I yearn for lies beyond my reach.

This foreign land, dear teacher, owns much wealth—
with cash all creature comforts can be bought.
I only lack a little thing or two:
my father's face, my mother's tender voice.

---

[1]   A Chinese Goddess of antiquity.
[2]   A Vietnamese famous poet in the late 19th century.

Imbibing her milk, I once grew up.
Under his roof I once became a man.
Her vast devotion matched the skies, the seas.
His love was like Mount Tan*, the river* Da.*³*

Vietnam, our land, is poor, an utter wretch,
but it gives us the taste of human love.
All its three parts share one stream of red blood.
How sweet it sounds, the lilt of our folk songs!

Bright moonlight over our Dong-thap, Nam-can.*⁴*
The waters of Dong-nai,*⁵ Beloved* Sai-gon.
The purple rice of Chau-doc *and* Long-xuyen.*⁶*
*What mountain boasts as many as Seven Hills?*⁷*

I loved to bet on horses whilst at school.
I flunked all subjects, history, civics, lit.
For homework I devoured those swordsmen's tales.
And now, too late, I rue my onetime sins.

---

³   The high mountain and big river in the North Vietnam.
⁴   Two big rice fields in the South Vietnam.
⁵   A river located in northwest of Saigon
⁶   Two provinces in Mekong River.
⁷   Vietnamese called "That Son", in Chau-Doc province.

By day, it's 'glorious' labor—eight full hours.
By night, I drown it all in acrid booze.
At learning why have I become a sloth?
I catch mere bits and shreds of their strange tongue.

If we're ill-bred, untutored, don't blame us,
because you never taught us one damn thing!
You championed Marx and Lenin both with zeal—
well, who has wrought such havoc in our land?

Goodbye for now, until we meet again.
Cheer up—don't feel so bad about it all.
The restive horse, whose legs have not worn out,
still hopes that someday he will gallop home.

(St. Louis, Dec. 22, 1978)

Translated by Huynh Sanh Thong

Spring Night Confidences

Is Spring really here, or is it only a dream?
Since I learned how to smile, I've waited for Spring.
Through thirty years of vagabond life,
I've heard Spring would free my shackled heart.

I know Spring rushes once it's come
with its liqueurs to fill souls to brimming.
But Oh what wretched, endless grief
this strange and frigid Spring imparts!

Spring sometimes idles as it comes,
then runs with no promise of returning.
Still, I pray and nourish faith
that Spring will return, smiles will set root.

I drink to Spring in these darkest times;
I chant my rhymes of hopeless waiting.
Spring, do you know? Oh what dreams I waste
on the buds of Love and Joy you've lost!

(Silver Spring, Jan. 23, 1981)

Translated from Vietnamese by R.S. Carlson

Life Candles

I'll blow out those red candles and observe

My birthday wandering in America.

Though quickly spring slips by, let me rejoice;

Time-stained, I've earned another year of age.

Here linger still two streams of candle tears;

They grieve and mourn that youth has inched away.

Mountains and oceans tear me roughly in two;

Half of my soul yet clings to my poor land.

And when I gaze toward it, my people seem

Outside the window flitting past like leaves.

Condemned to roll amidst the dust, I miss

Those left behind, long for my hills and streams.

I am a bird who's fled its crimson cage;

Wing-worn, it flies toward shores still lost in mists.

From my own people, shadows so remote,

Sad echoes of their whispers come at night.

Another birthday far away from home;

Much further yet I've strayed from native roots.

But on some happy day I'll be back there;

Awash with love, I'll celebrate my birth.

(Silver Spring, Sept. 6, 1981)

Translated from Vietnamese by Huynh Sanh Thong

Golda Meir

You're Special, Golda Meir

(Dedicated to Prime Minister Golda Meir)

Just wait 'til I tell you this story
'Bout you, Golda Meir, in all of your glory
I'm really impressed
By your vigor and zest
Israel is your territory.

Get ready to hear a great tale
For now, Golda Meir, it's you that I hail
You're fighting and persevering
And enduring and interesting
In Israel we look for your trail.

Your energy just seems to flow
You sure like to be on the go
You're darting and dashing
And fiery and flashing
So lively and busy you know.

Full of life like the sun's beaming rays
Energetically passing the days
You're vibrant and bright
And quite a delight
An energy deserving of praise.

You make an impression on me
You make me feel great as can be
Standing out from the rest
You're one of the best
You brighten my life now you see.

After you, they just threw out the mold
You're special -- more special than gold
You're one of a kind
Your heart and your mind
You're the first Prime Minister of the women's world.

(Germantown, May 1, 1986)

Happy Mother's Day

(To Mrs. Womble, Vellejo, CA)

The study has just been completed
It's you, Mother, who is to be greeted
So caring you are
More caring by far
In Vallejo you often are seated.

No one is as loving as you
You love me whatever I do
Like a hand to a glove
Is how you are to love
So perfectly matched are the two.

In ways that are loving and sharing
Yourself you give freely, not sparing
You love in a style
That's warm and worthwhile
Not selfish or narrow, just caring.

To care's your emotion preferred
To talk to you is to be heard
Inspired from above
You give of your love
In action, in thought, and in word.

As a mother you rank with the best
Your children are certainly blessed
You know when to free them
You know when to see them
And manage to do it with zest.

You're such a magnificent mother
A mother unique as no other
You know how to nourish
To make children flourish
Happy Mother's Day, World's Greatest Mother!

(Germantown, June 5, 1986)

Missing You

From Phoenix you go to-and-fro
I'll talk about you as I go
You love in a style
That's warm and worthwhile
It's you, my Lover, you know.

So loving, concerned, and good-hearted
From you I'll not want to be parted
You give yourself freely
The rewards of love from me
You get all the good feelings started.

I'm missing you more than you know
Where you are that's where I want to go
'Cause being with you
Brings joy through and through
When you're gone I just feel sort of low.

This feeling of emptiness started
Exactly the moment we parted
I'm sad and I'm blue
I'm sure missing you
Though life goes on I'm broken-hearted.

You'll tell all the truth so sincere
When you talk I'll believe what I hear
You're honest and swell
The truth you will tell
Integrity is your career.

I'm missing you now quite a bit
Your style, your ways, and your wit
Your family's grand
Impromptu or planned
I miss you a lot, I admit.

(Germantown, July 18, 1986)

Happy Mother's Day, Mother

(To Mrs. Alice Knudson, Clinton, Iowa)

This message to you, Mother, is real
It shows very well how I feel
You're loving and caring
Support you are sharing
In Clinton you live -- I reveal.

I heard quite an interesting rumor
Of you, Mother, told with much humor
You're honest and swell
The truth I can tell
In Clinton you're always a good mother.

You care about people sincerely
And bring others close very dearly
You're devoted and caring
So loving and sharing
Your love is expressed very clearly.

My love sometimes doesn't get spoken
I'm too busy to be a student
But now I can pause
And give some applause
Without you my heart would be broken.

So loving, concerned, and good-hearted
From you I'll not want to be parted
On Mother's Day
I want to say
You get all the good feelings started.

If mothers were rated and scored
You'd certainly get an award
This Mother's Day greeting
It bears some repeating
This mother deserves a reward!

(Germantown, September 19, 1986)

In Celebration of a June Wedding

Presented to the Weiss & Nguyen Families.
To Michael David and Brigitte Nguyet-Thu
with affectionate thought.

The flowers smile and butterflies hover in the Spring
When the Weiss and Nguyen families spread the good
*   news:*
The radiant bride Thu Nguyen
Will couple with a handsome groom
By the name of Michael Weiss
Scion of a distinguished American family...
O what a foresight the Matchmaker in the Moon had
When he tied up that marriage knot for a deserving
*   couple!*

***

Bride and Groom grew up in two different worlds
Who was to know what Heaven had in store for them?
East and West would never meet, they say,
But Love knows no boundary or limitation
As long as two hearts beat to the same beat
And to a same tune with an enchanting rhythm...
The parents are proud in front of the world
And the families find more and more drawn to each
    other
As long as husband and wife are of the same mind, the
    proverb says,
They can scoop up the Eastern Sea, whether in poverty
    or in wealth
For once they have exchanged marriage vows
They are bound to each other through thick and thin
Nothing, nothing will ever separate them:
The basis of Happiness, a Gift from Heaven.

***

Hail to a Vietnamese-Jewish alliance
That links two people who both love Peace
Each side keeping its own faith
But still finding there is room for a great love
Loving each other for their very ancestral roots—
For a tree must have roots, as a spring must have its
    source.
Together they will perpetuate the race
With love and kindness more important than gold
Tomorrow when their countries are proud again
Their wealth and might can only benefit both races and
    families...

***

The wine is barely touched and one is already
    inebriated
As we toast the bride, Thu Nguyen, on her wedding day:
Now that you are to join another family
Do not forget the love and bonding that your parents
    have given you
Do not forget, ever, your mother raising you
For this is a favor that no money will ever buy
Remember, my child, all that you have learned,
Industry, looks, judicious talk and behavior are always
    valid.

***

A toast also, I propose to Michael, the groom:
Now that you acquire a new family, make sure that all
*   goes well*
Be loving and thoughtful towards your wife
For nothing could best the ideal of Family Harmony...

***

A final toast, I would say, to both families:
Let the alliance be fruitful, leading to a long progeny...

A HUNDRED YEARS OF HAPPINESS TOGETHER
TO THE BRIDE AND THE GROOM

From Uncle Vinh-Liem and Aunt Thu-Ho
Your cousins Tram-Anh and Phuong-Anh

Germantown Residence
June 15, 1991
(4th day of the Fifth Lunar Month, Year of the Goat)

Translated from Vietnamese by Nguyen Ngoc Bich
(Springfield, VA)

My Mother

She's never tired. She'll never die.
She's too old but still alive.
I'm far from her, over twenty years;
She didn't know how I got here.

I'm too young to remember;
How my mother cares for her
Children. They live very far away;
She'll never know where I stay.

I have a mother—the only one;
She loves children and everyone.
She worked too hard—days and nights;
She's never tired, but smiles.

Lovely mother! What can I say?
You're in my heart everyday!

(Germantown, Feb. 9, 1998)

Peasant Woman

Enemy

It has no head, no eye, no mind;
It comes from my body—inside.
It has no leg, no hand, no arm;
It's not cold; it's not warm.

It has no house and no shelter;
It has nothing--brother or sister.
It has no relative and no family;
But I can feel and I can see.

It has no color and no race;
no identity and no birthplace.
Its body is a liquid form;
It's as harmful as a storm.

How often does it happen to me?
It's not my friend, but my enemy.

(Germantown, March 3, 1998)

Sorrow

(For Sophronia Holcomb)

It came out from inside suddenly with tears;
It bothers you, day and night, through fear.
It isn't black or white, green or blue;
It's a quite nightmare to be true.

You sit alone sometimes— try to remember;
What happens to your loved one—as a rumor!
Why not him?—God took him away!
Why not him?—What can you say?

What's a Heaven! What's a Hell!
Nobody knows! Who can tell?
Some life's too short; some life's long;
No one's equal; no dream as a song.

With that sorrow, you know how to feel;
For the moment, please don't yield!

(Germantown, March 19, 1998)

Farewell 20th Century!

Sad to say good-bye to you, 20th century!
Either you're slowing down or you're in a big hurry.
Time has passed. I don't wonder why;
You'll be gone; I'm still here—I try!

I'm suffering between rich and poor,
High class and poverty, young and old— on my door.
Where will you go while I stay here alone?
Your responsibility has not ended.

I lived throughout your industrial revolution;
With toxic, warm atmosphere, El nino, La nina, and
emotion.
Your last evolution with computer and information age;
Someone has to learn, someone hesitates.

I have enough nightmares and difficulties;
Throughout the war, there were many casualties!

(Germantown, March 19, 1998)

The Tet Offensive [1]

Happy New Year! Tet! Tet! Tet!
Food, wine, and beer. Let's celebrate!
Vietcong and Allied at the Cease Fire;
Wonderful fireworks in the blue sky.

Fireworks, drink, and sing until midnight;
Don't sleep. Await. Peace. Why fight?
Grenades, TNT, B-40's... had been found;
Machine guns placed somewhere in town.

Fire! Fire! Fire! Vietcong! Vietcong! Vietcong;
Death. Wounded. Ruined. Destroyed. Strong
Deadly rockets and bombs visited suddenly;
No ambulance. Darkness. High casualties.

Sorrow. Sadness. Widowed. Bad news.
Tet Offensive was a killing field!

(Germantown, March 3, 1998)

---

[1] 'Tet', in Vietnamese, means 'New Year'. The Tet Offensive in 1968

The Fall of Saigon

* Dedicated to the U.S. POWs & MIAs, Vietnam Veterans,
  and Vietnamese victims of the Vietnam War
* For Lt. Col. Samuel R. Shumaker, Ret., a veteran of two wars
  and a friend of Vietnamese
* For Ted Sampley, my dear friend

It's spring in 1975 -- a heaven or hell!
The war's strong. Terrible. I can tell.
Vietcong controlled over Central and Highlands;
Evacuated. Refugees. Fired. Ruined. No complaints!

CBU's over head. Dead enemy. Can't count;
Wounded. Death. Honest soldiers of the South.
Politics solutions had an arrangement;
Death of South Vietnam suddenly happened.

Vietcong and tanks surrounded Saigon. Rumor;
Defeated or blooded. Big Minh surrendered!
Armed Forces disintegrated. People had to flee;
Anywhere. Any means out the country.

Vietcong invaded Saigon. There's no 'enemy';
Suddenly they celebrated a victory!

(Germantown, March 7, 1998)

An Honest Soldier

(For Lt. Col. Samuel R. Shumaker, Ret.)

Fifty years, that far in memory,
Either in Marine Corps or Army.
Served nation, people, and justice;
Proud of you. Honestly. Interested!

You never die! Your heart and your mind;
Strong. Intelligent. Clear as blue sky.
Fight for Freedom, Human Rights--Citizen!
Your love, your duty for the United Nations.

You're bright as a star;
What you did in the past, so far.
Wounded. Stand up. Fighting. Prison.
You did a good job! Proud of you, citizen!

War. Duty. Honest soldier.
Back to your duty. Do not retire, Colonel!

(Germantown, March 2, 1998)

The War

Every single day is a living war!
It's not too close. It's not too far.
Twenty-four hours in a battlefield;
Some live; others are killed.

A baby born in a warm atmosphere;
He cries while his parents cheer.
He wonders what's happened or is he scared?
Nobody knows! Nobody cares!

As a teenager he has to learn;
Something he loses; something he earns.
For his future he has built up his mind;
His attitude, and his behavior inside.

To survive in the long run;
He has to fight and has no fun.

(Germantown, March 3, 1998)

The War (II)

(For Lt. Col. Samuel R. Shumaker, Ret.)

Ruined. Evacuated. Wounded. Casualties.
Bombs. Rockets. Both sides – Allied, enemy.
Icy roads. Tanks. Trucks. Jeeps...
Wide opened eyes. Nobody could sleep!

Storm. Snow. Air drops. Convoys. Cargo.
Ambulance. Medical supplies. Dead soldiers...
Hospitals. Battle ships. Refugees.
Marine Corps. Air Forces. Army. Navy.

Parachutes. Fights. The terrible cold!
Long road to hell! Soldiers. Unknown.
Peace. Justice. Nightmare.
Communists. Freedom. Who cares?

Is that a war? War! War! War!
Nobody knows. It's too far.

(Germantown, March 3, 1998)

Inspiration (II)

(For Ryelynn Johnson)

'I was too young to get married.'
When I asked her 'Why weren't you interested?
'Because I couldn't find the right one.
I was still young; I liked to be alone.'

She surprised me— she's still single;
Does she ever feel she is alone?
She has pretty smiles—days and nights;
They inspire me—I have no surprises.

I fell in love, but how can I tell?
All long nights, I live in the hell.
Her images bother me a lot;
What can I say? Why can I not?

Although I am a married man
I fell in love with a single woman.

(Bethesda, November 8, 1999)

Puberty

The Silent Love

(For Ryelynn Johnson)

She and I fell in love with each other.
We are the new romantic lovers.
She sits at the other side of the building.
She loves her job; it's interesting.

We never say: 'I love you' to each other;
But she and I— both are two partners.
We keep silence in our sweet hearts.
That's true love; but we don't go too far.

I work too hard on the electronic mail.
She replies quickly, all questions in detail.
We laugh and love the silent love.
That's fantastic! She's quiet as a dove.

As long as we still fall in love with each other.
We keep silent. Nobody knows we're partners.

(Bethesda, November 9, 1999)

My Sweet Heart

(For Ryelynn Johnson)

She always called me, 'My sweet heart;'
I have no idea, but my love, so far.
She's modest, nice, and sweet;
That's what I like and what I need.

She cares for me and I care for her;
She's younger than me–I'm sure.
She enjoys her life as a single lady;
No child, no anguish, and no anxiety...

I wish I were always her sweet heart in her life;
Either I passed away or I am still alive.
I am her sweet heart for two centuries;
Is it too long? Will she be happy?

I am glad to be her sweet heart;
Oh my lover! You're a great recreation park.

(Bethesda, November 10, 1999)

Love

(For Ryelynn Johnson)

Love is the life of nature and human;
Without love, there are many pains.
In our modern society, crime is an example;
Without love, there are no people.

Love is seen anywhere, in any kind;
Love is natural; it is found in the mankind...
Love is needed as the fresh air;
You can feel and you can share.

Love is green and love is blue;
Without love, nothing else is true.
We need love the same as we need food;
Love is gold because love is good...

My love for her is a normal love;
We play, enjoy, and breathe as a dove.

(Bethesda, November 11, 1999)

Sorrow (II)

(Dedicated to Brad Marggraff, Germantown, MD)

Suddenly I hear the bad news of the day;
My neighbor — also a friend – just passed away.
He's nice and handsome; he's a good man;
Why do you die so young, my dear friend?

You have lovely children – both young girls;
A beautiful wife and a free world.
Over fifteen years in the same place and
     neighborhood;
We all love and enjoy the good food.

We love you and we miss you;
God takes you away – is that true?
Thanksgiving is less than a week from today;
We pray for you, my dear friend, anyway.

God Bless your family – your children and your wife;
Take your time to celebrate a new life.

(Germantown, November 19, 1999)

My Neighbor

(For Ryelynn Johnson)

She was young and pretty at that time;
I met her and loved her – she was mine.
She gave births to my two daughters;
I thought she loved me forever.

We have two beautiful girls and a house;
We have a good family, yet I am proud.
I work hard because I am the bread winner;
She spends all her times at home as a babysitter.

One day she said she has made her decision;
I don't know why she wanted a separation.
We live in the same house, treat each other as
     neighbors;
She has her own life – I feel like a stranger.

My love is hard and my life is tough!
Why isn't my love for her enough?

(Germantown, November 24, 1999)

Tune Up

(For Ryelynn Johnson)

I'm as a ten-year-old engine without a tune up;
I have a wife but her love is down and up.
Sometimes she's nice; sometimes she's mad;
I gave her my love; she never gave it back.

I'm her husband and she's my wife;
We live same house; there are different lives.
She goes to the north; I go to the south;
She thinks she will go up and I will go down.

We never love though we don't have to tune up;
She's cold; her voice is sour as ketchup.
I live with her; yet I'm always alone;
It's a nightmare. I don't know how to solve!

Someone advises me – change my life style;
Divorce the old one and find a new wife.

(Germantown, November 24, 1999)

I'm Feeling Blue

(For Ryelynn Johnson)

One day you said, 'I'm feeling blue!'
From your heart, I think it's true.
You're a wonderful woman, my young lady!
You care for your parents because they're your family.

I hope your father will be fine;
He's really sick but he's still alive.
He wants to stay at home with his children;
I pray for him at this moment!

I know someday he will pass away;
What will you feel? What would you say?
You'll be crying for him as a young child
But he'll never be far away from your mind.

Be proud of your father--he's a good man;
You're always a young girl, my dear friend!

(Germantown, Dec. 5, 2000)

The Pentagon At Risk

(Respectfully dedicated to the victims of the
hijackers at the Pentagon, Sept. 11, 2001)

An airplane suddenly jumps into the Pentagon;
Causing a series of explosions and destruction.
Sending up a plume of smoke into the blue sky;
The Potomac River and the Pentagon City are very
*   quiet.*

Nobody knows this moment in the great country;
Because of its tolerance and diversity.
Killing all onboard and other members of the
*   Pentagon;*
This brutal attack is enormous and depraved!

The deadly crash by the acts of terror!
The terrible attack by the suicide hijackers.
Causing great loss of life and tremendous damage;
The evildoers to be severely executed and punished.

We mourn with those who have suffered great loss;
The perpetrators must be brought to justice at any
*   costs.*

(Germantown, Sept. 11,2001)

Suicide In The Sky

(Respectfully dedicated to the victims of the
 hijackers in New York City, Sept. 11, 2001)

Suddenly the airplanes crashed into the twin towers.
They're exploded. A huge plume of smoke... No
*   power...*
The skyscrapers are made by the forged steel;
Oh my God! It's really hot! How do they feel?

Who are you—my crazy young men?
Why do you want to kill our dear friends?
You are too young! You must save your lives!
Why do you want to commit suicide?

The killers did prepare for their threats;
Nobody knows that action in their heads.
How many people were burned in that site?
Oh my God! It was a terrible suicide!

Hijackers are not only our real enemy;
They are Satans of many countries.

(Germantown, 9-11-2001)

American Flag

What's the American flag, my dear friends?
What do you think about your flag in common sense?
Should you keep it in your warmest heart?
As your favorite thing and with your best regards.

I saw you used the American flag as a hat;
You used it as a necktie and a bath towel.
You used it as a swimming suit and as trousers;
You used it anywhere and for whatever.

My American flag is a supernatural power;
I can't make it as pants or trousers!
It should be flying, always, over my head;
I can't make it as a T-shirt or a bath towel.

My American flag, to me, is a supernatural moral;
I lover it, respect it, and am proud of it. My American
    fellows!

(Germantown, Sept. 25, 2001)

Air Strikes

Honey! Are fireworks lighting up the Afghan midnight
*   sky?*
Oh! No. The United States is launching the air strikes.
She reserves the right, I think, to strike at terrorist
*   cells;*
So bin Laden and his members are fleeing to the hell.

Cruise missiles and unguided bombs attack Taliban's
*   missile sites;*
Many of the bombs were guided by our satellites.
Destroying Taliban's airfields, aircraft, radars,
*   training camps...*
That's the conventional military campaign's aim.

Heavy bombers and supersonic jets are all over
*   Afghanistan—*
Terrorist targets. Though food and medicine for
*   humanitarian needs.*
Honey! Do you think America will win this strange war?
What do you mean, Honey? The bin Laden terrorist
*   war?*

Yes, we're working to bring the evil-doers to justice;
That's why the military action is designed to bring the
*   battle to the terrorists.*

(Germantown, Oct. 7, 2001)

Dream

Women For Sale

Did you ever buy a young woman for six thousand
   dollars?
Viet communists are doing this business, as a trade too
   far!
You can find their ad on the eBay website; [1]
You can buy these young ladies, if you don't mind.

Most of these modern slaves are beautiful and young;
They're the victims of Viet communist gangs.
They're poor, but Viet communists are very rich;
That's a communist world—They do what they need.

My heart is broken when I see that Web page!
But some Taiwanese were all ready to purchase.
They bought a young slave with a price that was very
   cheap!
How did they feel? How long will they keep?

That's a new business in Vietnam today!
Please don't do that dirty business with communists!
   OK?

(Germantown, March 5, 2004)

---

[1]   This ad was removed from eBay website on March 6, 2004.

Congratulations!

(For Tram-Anh, my daughter)

You'll graduate on the 20th of May, 2004,
You'll get what you deserved –
After five years in college and hard study –
A Bachelor degree in Information Technology.

I'm proud of you! My lovely daughter,
A good student and citizen forever.
The United States is your beautiful country,
Love her and protect her honestly.

I've learned that Clifton Gunderson
offers you an IT position this month.
It's is your first job in a consulting firm.
I'm glad to hear that! — You did confirm.

Everyone will respect you as an engineer,
Keep a good faith! Good luck on your new job, my dear!

(Germantown, May 15, 2004)

Farewell Mr. President

(Respectfully dedicated to Mr. Ronald Wilson Reagan)

Sad news on the radio touched my heart deeply
On the way I'm going to a wedding party.
You've just passed away from your hometown;
It's far away! Please don't let me down!

You touched my heart and your people's hearts;
It's raining today—it's windy and very dark.
A farewell to you because you're gone;
You left your lovely Nancy here alone.

You helped us have a good life and a rich America;
A wonderful history: the Berlin Wall and the Star War.
Your enemy—Mr. Gorbachev—became your friend;
You did a very good job as the United States' president.

You're going to heaven for a new life;
I miss you because I cannot say 'goodbye'!

(Germantown, June 5, 2004)

July Fourth

*Sitting here on a lovely night to watch the fireworks in
    the dark sky;*
Hoping everybody enjoys Independence Day tonight.
Something to drink? Oh yes! Spring water or mineral;
*I thirst as our fathers did when they fought for their
    goals.*

Independence for our nation is not cheap;
*Blood, bodies, bone, families, assets – these they
    couldn't keep.*
But their souls are still alive forever in our lives;
Lovely Country, wonderful people together tonight.

Everybody came here for their fresh Liberty;
Living here they're not afraid of their enemy.
Keeping life for their children's future;
Education is a primary goal – I'm sure.

To celebrate July Fourth is a pride of our citizens;
*For keeping our Country beautiful and preserving its
    Independence.*

(Germantown, July 4, 2005)

New Life in the United States

Specially dedicated to Mr. Cao and his family members.
The thirtieth anniversary of his family's settlement in the U.S.

Imagine how it feels to start a new life in the United
*   States!*
As refugees we're all strangers and new faces.
We did not own assets or money;
Nothing! But fresh hearts and family.

Learning a new life is not easy for adults;
Slower than young men to get the results.
English is a hard barrier to overcome in our lives;
How can we learn it fast in a night!

Everyday we think about a new career;
How to find it and get it within a year.
Our young children must be sent to a new school;
Starting over a new life is my primary goal.

Our motherland now is far away from my sight;
But my heart still loves her every night.

(Germantown, July 4, 2005)

Katrina – A Nightmare

(Respectfully dedicated to the victims of
Hurricane Katrina in Louisiana and Mississippi)

Katrina! You're the strongest lady I've ever seen!
How can I describe the powerful hurricane you have
    been!
You destroyed everything in New Orleans city
And took thousands of lives from those families!

Why did you choose Mississippi and Louisiana?
These states are wonderful, Katrina!
You came over and left them a mess,
Your action has caused distress!

Two Astro Domes did not have enough spaces for
    refugees,
Flood waters still cover all the cities.
Food and fresh water are all a shortage!
How will these people survive? They're shelterless!

Katrina! Our people have lived in a terrific nightmare!
Your name is beautiful but we don't care.

(Germantown, September 2, 2005)

Farewell Dr. Hoang Thien Can

Respectfully dedicated to the memory of Dr. Hoang Thien Can.
For Mrs. Minh Ha, his widow, with deepest sympathy.

A sad news suddenly broke my heart today!
I feel very sad about it! What can I say?
A funeral was set forth Dr. Hoang Thien Can,
Both Friday and Saturday, I'll come, if I can.

I've owned his helpful advice and his family
Since he helped me to entertain our dinner parties.
He always helped our community when needed.
He never said any complaints or disbursal indeed.

He's not only a physician, but also an artist,
He loved painting, song, and music.
His wife, Minh Ha, was his loyal partner,
She's a beautiful wife and a famous singer.

How can I say enough about this great man?
What I can say is, farewell, my dear friend!

(Germantown, June 7, 2006)

Have a good time, pay a high price

(To remember a terrible night – August 6, 2006)

It's a brightest day and a lovely night.
Surrounded by old friends, we'd a very good time.
Talking. Laughing. Security and election year;
Politics. Nobody knows; nobody fears.

I can drive. Don't worry. I'll be home, honey!
Where's my wallet? Where're my keys?
Oh! Fresh air, a lovely night!
I drove slowly, but I had two flat tires!

What can I do? My eyes are blown;
Oh! MC campus – the sign is shown.
Parking lot is not far, you must reach there.
Nobody knows; nobody cares.

Suddenly a police officer stopped by.
As a result, I got tickets for DWI!

(Germantown, October 21, 2006)

'Seven Locks Hotel'

(To remember my first 'vacation' at S.L. Detention Center for DUI)

I arrived at 'Seven Locks Hotel' at six o'clock p.m.
My 'weekend vacation' for twelve days – sentences – at
*   a special camp.*
Wait and see what'll happen tonight;
I have nothing to say. Surrounded by strangers with
*   red eyes.*

Sitting in the visiting room until 7:44;
Screening procedures take 4 hours or more.
I'm nude in front of a policeman's eye;
To change clothes in dark gray uniform, he never
*   minds.*

All weekenders surrounded by uniform policemen with
*   many keys;*
As taxpayers we keep them busy and pay them high
*   salary.*
No matter who we are – They trust us as prisoners;
Literally and courteously – they call us weekenders.

Three meals per day as same as Marriott Hotel;
All meals and lodging only fifteen dollars are not bad!
*   I can tell.*

(Rockville, 12/15/2006)

Good-bye, my old friend!

(Farewell Mr. Alcohol)

You're my old friend for a long time
But you bothered me and shook my life!
You spent a lot of my money
And my time – that's a main key.

There were three times you made me hurt
While I chat with my friends in Falls Church
You asked me to drink a lot of beer
And made me keep going to cheer.

The second time I was in Gaithersburg
With some friends, you told me that it wouldn't hurt.
The third time, in Clarksburg, you gave me more
    than five –
One shot of whisky and five glasses of wine.

Finally, I got total three tickets for DUI!
You're my enemy, Mr. Alcohol! I must say good-bye!

(Germantown, April 2, 2007)

My Twelve Steps
(The Process of Recovery)

I've learned that my life under alcohol is
        unmanageable;
Following the twelve steps is my daily bible.
My body is powerless over alcohol [1] – I admit it;
I believe that it is a Power greater than myself [2] –
        that's it.

My decision is to turn my will and life over to the care
        of God; [3]
Every day I make a moral inventory of myself [4] – what
        I've got.
Admitted to God and to myself that my wrongs are the
        exact nature of drink; [5]
I'm ready to have God remove all these defects of
        character. [6]

---

[1]   Step One
[2]   Step Two
[3]   Step Three
[4]   Step Four
[5]   Step Five
[6]   Step Six

Humbly I ask Him to remove my shortcomings; [7]
I make a list of all persons I had harmed [8] *– I'm willing*
to make direct amends to them wherever possible, but
            would not injure them; [9]
Continue to take personal inventory and admit to
            doing the same. [10]

Praying for knowledge of His will for me and the power
            to carry that out; [11]
I try to carry these messages and principles to all
            alcoholics, I'm proud. [12]

(Germantown, 10-31-2007)

---

[7]   Step Seven
[8]   Step Eight
[9]   Step Nine
[10] Step Ten
[11] Step Eleven
[12] Step Twelve

Sorrow (III)

Dedicated to the memory of Angela Lucas (01.08.07 – 03.16.08)
For Sarah Moran, her mother, with deepest sympathy.

Suddenly I heard some bad news today,
Angela Lucas passed away on Sunday.
She never woke up after a long sleep in the afternoon,
Nobody knows why she's gone so soon?

What happened to her, my dear friend?
She was healthy. Why has she died? I don't
understand.
Last Friday in my living room, she played with a lot of
toys.
She smiled, talked, and ate her food that she enjoyed.

She was intelligent. Maybe a bright student – grade A;
Maybe be a good doctor or a famous lawyer, I would
say.
Why has she abandoned her life so very soon?
In a long sleep in that Sunday afternoon.

With my deepest sympathy, and my family on my side;
Best wishes for you – Angela – in Heaven's new life!

(Germantown, 03-17-2008)

VINH LIEM'S WORKS OF ART AND TECHNICAL

BOOKS PUBLISHED IN VIETNAM

BOOK OF POEMS
1. *'Tho Vinh Liem'* (Vinh Liem's Poems) written in Vietnamese, published in 1974

BOOKS READY FOR PUBLICATION IN VIETNAM ALL WORKS FELL INTO COMMUNIST HANDS AND WERE DESTROYED

A. BOOKS OF POEMS (1964-1975) written in Vietnamese
1. *'Loi Tu Tinh Cua Bien'* (The Ocean's Whispering)
2. *'Tu Thu'* (Confession)
3. *'Que Huong Trong Trai Tim Nguoi'* (The Native Land In One's Heart)
4. *'Coi Doi Hiu Quanh'* (The Deserted Life)
5. *'Cat Vang'* (The Yellow Sands)

B. COLLECTIONS OF SHORT STORIES (1964-1975) written in Vietnamese
1. *'Mua Xuan Cua Nang'* (The Spring of Her Life)
2. *'Loi Thoat'* (The Way Out)
3. *'Que Nha'* (Fatherland)

C. NOVEL (1970-1975) written in Vietnamese
1. *'Go Cua Tinh Yeu'* (The First Love)

BOOKS WERE PUBLISHED IN THE UNITED STATES

A. BOOKS OF POEMS
1. *'Ti Nan Truong Ca,' Tap I* (Refugee's Confidences), Vol. I, book of poems written in Vietnamese, published in 1980
2. *'Bi Ca Nguoi Vuot Bien'* (Lament of the Boat People), book of poems written in Vietnamese, published in 1980

3. *'Ti Nan Truong Ca,' Tap II* (Refugee's Confidences), Vol. II, book of poems written in Vietnamese, published in 1982
4. *'Without Beginning, Without End'* in English, published in 2008

B. COLLECTION OF SHORT STORIES
1. *'Ga Ti Nan'* (The Refugee Guy), a collection of short stories written in Vietnamese, published in 1986

BOOKS READY FOR PUBLICATION

A. BOOKS OF POEMS (in English and Vietnamese language)
1. *'Ti Nan Truong Ca,' Tap III* (Refugee's Confidences), Vol. III, written in Vietnamese
2. *'Ti Nan Truong Ca,' Tap IV* (Refugee's Confidences), Vol. IV, written in Vietnamese
3. *'Ti Nan Truong Ca,' Tap V* (Refugee's Confidences), Vol. V, written in Vietnamese
4. *'Ti Nan Truong Ca,' Tap VI* (Refugee's Confidences), Vol. VI, written in Vietnamese
5. *'Ti Nan Truong Ca,' Tap VII* (Refugee's Confidences), Vol. VII, written in Vietnamese
6. *'Huong Dong Noi'* (Country's Fragrance) written in Vietnamese
7. *'Thang Hoa'* (Sublimation) written in Vietnamese
8. *'Con Vuong To Long'* (Ties of Affection) written in Vietnamese
9. *'Lament of The Boat People'* in English

B. COLLECTIONS OF SHORT STORIES (written in Vietnamese)
1. *'Hanh Phuc Phia Ben Kia'* (Motherland's Happiness)
2. *'Ngay Xuan Chua Du Am'* (The Springtime Without Happiness)
3. *'Hoi Huong'* (Repatriation)

C. MUSIC/SONGS/THEATER (written in Vietnamese)
1. *'Thuyen Tinh'* (Boat of Love), collection of songs
2. *'Nhat Dinh Thang'* (Decided Victory*),* collection of songs
3. *'Co Nhac Viet Nam'* (Vietnamese Renovated Theater and Traditional Music`)`

D. LITERATURE (written in Vietnamese)
1. *'Vuon Hoa Van Hoc'* (Garden of Literature – Vietnamese Writers Overseas: Works and Authors)
2. *'Tha Huong Van Tap'* (Confidences on the foreign country)
3. *'Huong Sac Trong Vuon Tho'* (Fragrance in the Poetry Corner)

E. RELIGION (written in Vietnamese)
1. *'Nep Song Hoa-Hao'* (Hoa-Hao Buddhism's Life)

F. POLITICS (written in Vietnamese)
1. *'The Luc Nao?'* (What's Influence?)
2. *'Tuyen Tap Can Bo'* (Political Cadre's Handbook)

G. COLLECTIONS OF ESSAYS (written in Vietnamese)
1. *'Chuyen Ben Le'* (The Sideline's Stories)
2. *'Nguoc Gio'* (Up The Wind) – an idle talk
3. *'Minh Oi!'* (My Dear!) – comic stories

H. COLLECTIONS OF ESSAYS (in English)
1. *'Two Faces of Life'*

I. BUSINESS, ECONOMICS, & FINANCE (in English)
1. *'Loan Officer's Handbook'*
2. *'Mortgage Processor's Handbook'*
3. *'Dictionary of Real Estate and Mortgage'*
4. *'New Vietnam, Great Opportunities'*
5. *'Real Estate and Mortgage Markets in Vietnam'*

Contact Information:
Email: vinhliem9@hotmail.com
Home Page: http://vinhliem.tripod.com

$14.95 USA / $18.95 CAN

Vinh Liem was born in South Vietnam in 1944. He joined the Vietnamese Navy in 1964. After the fall of South Vietnam, he fled his country and eventually settled in the United States in September 1975.

Vinh Liem has been a poet, writer and journalist since 1964 and between 1980 and 1986, he published four books of poems and short stories in the United States.

Vinh Liem's poems have also been published by several respected organizations and magazines, including the Vietnamese Pen Club Overseas ('War and Exile' 1987); The National Library of Poetry in Owings Mills, Maryland ('A Break In The Clouds' 1993, 'At Day's End' 1994, and 'Divining Beauty' 2001). British publishers, Noble House, published the 'Theatre of the Mind' in 2003. One poem ('Enemy') was recorded in *'The Sound of Poetry'*, released both on compact disk and cassette tape in Fall 2001, by The International Library of Poetry.

Since the fall of South Vietnam in 1975, Vinh Liem has contributed to many Vietnamese newspapers and magazines in the United States, as well as publications in Canada, Europe, Asia, and Australia.

From 1979 to 1981, Vinh Liem was the managing editor of *Hanh Trinh* magazine and the *Hanh Dong* newspaper in Washington, D.C. He has also been the editor-in-chief of *The Vietnam Times* (Washington, D.C.) from 1984 to 1985, and the *Sao Trang* magazine (Miami, FL) from 1992 to 1994.

www.ingramcontent.com/pod-product-compliance
Lightning Source LLC
LaVergne TN
LVHW091208080426
835509LV00006B/887